# BRAIN BOOSTERS
# ADDING AND SUBTRACTING
## ACTIVITY BOOK

ARCTURUS

ARCTURUS

This edition published in 2019 by
Arcturus Publishing Limited
26/27 Bickels Yard, 151–153 Bermondsey Street,
London SE1 3HA

Written by: Penny Worms
Illustrated and designed by: Graham Rich
Consultant: Amanda Rock
Thunderpanda Font by Eric Wirjanata.
www.thunderpanda.com

ISBN: 978-1-78950-604-4
CH006948NT
Supplier 29, Date 0519, Print Run 8729

Printed in China

# CONTENTS

# WHAT IS ADDING?

Adding is a quick way of calculating the total of two (or more) amounts. It's much faster than counting. Here's Whiz-Bang the Wizard adding up his rabbits.

> I had one rabbit. Now I have four more. That means I have five rabbits!

As an equation, it looks like this:

$$1 + 4 = 5$$

Adding bigger numbers can be so hard that, unless you are a number wizard like Whiz-Bang, you need to calculate the equations on a piece of paper.

> Shh! Here's a secret. Sometimes I write down equations!

$$421 + 538 = 959$$

Easy or hard, there are a number of ways you can add numbers, and you'll be shown many of them in this book.

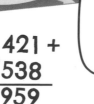

```
421 +
538
―――
959
```

# WHAT IS SUBTRACTING?

Subtracting is the opposite of adding. It's a way of finding out how many of something you have after some are taken away.

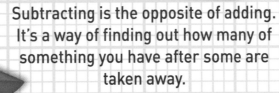

I had five rabbits. Now I have only one!

As an equation, it looks like this:

$$5 - 4 = 1$$

Subtracting is the INVERSE of adding, which just means you do the opposite.

So if **68 + 7 = 75**

Then **75 - 7 = 68**

You'll be a number wizard in no time!

Can you do this one?

**34 + 9 = 43**

**43 - 9 =**

GREAT WORK!

# ADDING IN ACTION

Whiz-Bang has lined up his wands to make a "number line," a line of numbers placed in their correct position. Number lines are great for adding single numbers (units).

To do the equation **4 + 3**, start at **4** and COUNT ON **3**.

+ 1    2    3

1   2   3   4   5   6   7   8   9   10

So, **4 + 3 = 7**

Number lines can start and end with any numbers.
Try the equation 37 + 3 using this number line.

34   35   36   37   38   39   40   41   42   43

"Counting on" is a magic method. You can try it again on page 10.

All the answers are at the end of the book.

**37 + 3 =** ☐

# MAGIC MEANINGS

When you see an equation like this:

**4 + 2**

It means:

Four **PLUS** two
**ADD** four and two
Four **INCREASED BY** two
The **TOTAL** of four and two
Four and two **EQUALS**

THEY ALL MEAN THE SAME!

And the answer is **6**!

When you see the **+** sign, you know you have to add up.

READY TO DO SOME ADDING?

7

# ADDING ONE

Merlin Mouse needs to collect 10 berries. He can only carry one at a time. Here is a snapshot of his day so far. Fill in the other answers.

1 + 1 = 2        4 + 1 = ☐

2 + 1 = ☐        5 + 1 = ☐

3 + 1 = ☐        6 + 1 = ☐

Here is his pile of berries. He is coming back with one more. How many berries will he have then?

7 + 1 = ☐

How many more trips will he need to make before he has 10 and can take a nap? ☐

ADD 1

Help Merlin with these equations, too. Fill in the missing numbers.

13 + 1 = ☐

☐ + 1 = 11

25 + 1 = ☐

31 + 1 = ☐

☐ + 1 = 4

59 + 1 = ☐

☐ + 1 = 100

199 + 1 = ☐

222 + ☐ = 223

Can you do these equations in your head?

All the answers are at the end of the book.

READY FOR MORE?

# COUNTING ON

"Counting on" just means to count forward. For example, 3 + 2 is easy. You count on 2 from 3, so you go 3 ... 4 ... 5! It's a great method when adding units (1 to 9), especially since you can use your fingers as a number line.

Try these equations by counting on.

$4 + 3 =$ ☐

$0 + 2 =$ ☐

$4 + 4 =$ ☐

$8 + 4 =$ ☐

$5 + 1 =$ ☐

Merlin has lots of brothers and sisters. How many are in each photograph?

MY BROTHERS ☐

MY SISTERS ☐

How many in total? ☐

# MERLIN MOUSE'S EQUATIONS

Help Merlin with these equations. Fill in the gaps.

Count on your fingers to check your answers.

$6 + 4 =$ ☐

$10 +$ ☐ $= 16$     $21 + 9 =$ ☐

$16 + 3 =$ ☐     $52 +$ ☐ $= 54$

$5 +$ ☐ $= 5$     $48 + 2 =$ ☐

When you are adding, it doesn't matter which way around the equation goes. The answer to $53 + 5$ is the same as $5 + 53$. So you can "count on" 5 starting at 53. Write the answer here:

$5 + 53 =$ ☐

Now try these equations:

$1 + 101 =$ ☐     $8 + 35 =$ ☐

NOW TEST YOURSELF WITH SOME FUN PUZZLES.

11

# MERLIN MOUSE'S BRAIN-TEASERS

Merlin is playing with three of his brothers. Five more come outside to play. How many is he playing with now?

Yum-yum!

Merlin's found **5** chunks of cheese in the kitchen. Then he finds **2** more. How many chunks of cheese does he have?

One of these is NOT a term that means "add." Circle it.

PLUS   +   PRODUCT   TOTAL   INCREASE

Merlin is **2** years old.
How old will he be in **4** years?

Merlin and his sister Mudge are playing a game.
They get **2** points every time they roll a ball into a
bucket and **5** points every time they roll it through
the mouse hole in the wall.

Here are their scores:

|  | Merlin | Mudge |
|---|---|---|
| Bucket | 2 | 1 |
| Hole | 1 | 2 |

**Points**

Who has won the game?...................................

NOW YOU KNOW HOW TO COUNT ON!

# SUBTRACTION IN ACTION

Here are Whiz-Bang's wands again to show you how to subtract by counting back. Number lines are useful when subtracting single numbers (units).

To do the equation **4 - 3**, start at **4** and COUNT BACK **3**.

3  2  1  -

1  2  3  4  5  6  7  8  9  10

So, **4 - 3 = 1**

Just like counting on, it doesn't matter where the number line begins. Try the equation below, using the number line.

25  26  27  28  29  30  31  32  33

**Counting back is the INVERSE (opposite) of counting on.**

**33 - 5 =** ☐

# MAGIC MEANINGS

THEY ALL MEAN THE SAME!

When you see an equation like this: **5 - 3**

It means:

Five **SUBTRACT** three

Five **TAKE AWAY** three

Five **MINUS** three

Five **DECREASED** by three

Five **LESS** three

The **DIFFERENCE** between five and three

And the answer is **2**!

When you see the ━ sign, you know you have to take away.

READY TO SUBTRACT?

# TAKE AWAY ONE

Kit Cat is eating treats. She has 8 in her bowl, and she eats one at a time. Count back with her.

8 - 1 = ☐

7 - 1 = ☐

6 - 1 = ☐

5 - 1 = ☐

4 - 1 = ☐

3 - 1 = ☐

2 - 1 = ☐

Kit is now sad. After she eats the next one, how many will she have left? ☐

# MORE THAN TEN

Kit can take away from double and triple digits!

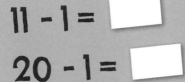

$11 - 1 =$ ☐

$20 - 1 =$ ☐

☐ $- 1 = 23$

$13 - 1 =$ ☐

☐ $- 1 = 20$

$32 - 1 =$ ☐

☐ $- 1 = 0$

$100 - 1 =$ ☐

$101 - 1 =$ ☐

I count back in my head.

READY FOR SOME MORE?

# COUNTING BACK

Kit Cat likes doing easy equations by counting back. For you, it is even easier since you can use your fingers to help you.

4 - 1 =

6 - 2 =

10 - 5 =

8 - 4 =

9 - 6 =

Here are three bowls of cat treats. If Kit eats three treats from each bowl, how many will be left? Cross out three to find out (the first one has been done for you).

7 - 3 = 4

10 - 3 =

4 - 3 =

# COUNT BACK WITH KIT CAT

Now try these equations.

$9 - 2 =$ ☐

$10 -$ ☐ $= 2$

$26 - 5 =$ ☐

$8 -$ ☐ $= 1$

$32 - 3 =$ ☐

$68 -$ ☐ $= 59$

$22 - 2 =$ ☐

$13 -$ ☐ $= 8$

$80 - 7 =$ ☐

Use your fingers as a number line.

Unlike adding, it DOES matter which way around the equation goes when you are subtracting. The answer to $2 - 1$ is not the same as $1 - 2$. If you have two apples and you eat one, you have one left. But if you have one apple, you cannot eat two!

NOW TEST YOURSELF WITH SOME FUN PUZZLES.

# KIT CAT'S BRAIN-TEASERS

Kit and her friend Claudius are watching birds in the garden. There are **5** birds, but **3** fly away.
How many are left?

Kit has **5** toys. Claudius has one less than Kit. How many toys does Claudius have?

Take away **5** from **6**.

Circle the term that does NOT mean subtract.

MINUS - INCREASE TAKEAWAY DECREASE

Kit has made **20** muddy paw prints on the kitchen floor.
Her owner has mopped up **8** already.
How many are left?

Like all cats, Kit and Claudius were both born with **9** lives.
Kit has lost **2**, and Claudius has lost **4**.
How many do they each have left?

Kit ◯        Claudius ◯

If **6** is **8** decreased by **2**,
what is **9** decreased by **3**?

You are a clever cat!

Subtract **1** from **6**.

NOW YOU KNOW HOW TO COUNT BACK!

# REMEMBER IT!

Ready for a recap on how to add and subtract units by counting on and back?

Try doing them in your head, but if you need to, use a number line or your fingers to help you.

$11 + 3 = \boxed{\phantom{00}}$

$90 - 2 = \boxed{\phantom{00}}$

$\boxed{\phantom{00}} + 5 = 10$

$18 + \boxed{\phantom{00}} = 26$

$3 - \boxed{\phantom{00}} = 0$

Whiz-Bang has **4** wands in his hand. If he decreases that number by **3**, how many wands will he be holding? $\boxed{\phantom{00}}$

Whiz-Bang is making potions. He has made **10** but needs to increase that number by **5**. How many potions will he have? $\boxed{\phantom{00}}$

Merlin had **10** berries. He eats **3**, and then he eats another **2**. Cross them out to find out how many he has left.

10 - 3 - 2 =

Merlin is playing hide-and-seek with his **8** brothers and **8** sisters. He has found **3** of them. How many more does he need to find?

Kit is making more muddy paw prints. She has taken **14** steps. How many paw prints will there be if she takes another?

**3** steps?

**7** steps?

WELL DONE! YOU ARE GREAT!

23

# NUMBER BONDS TO 10

Knowing number bonds is very handy!

A hook?

Pirate Blacktooth knows all the numbers that add up to 10. Here they are. These are called "number bonds," so learn them well!

$$9 + 1 = 10$$
$$8 + 2 = 10$$
$$7 + 3 = 10$$
$$6 + 4 = 10$$
$$5 + 5 = 10$$
$$4 + 6 = 10$$
$$3 + 7 = 10$$
$$2 + 8 = 10$$
$$1 + 9 = 10$$

# LEARNING NUMBER BONDS

When you know your number bonds, it makes adding easier.
Connect the coins that add up to **10**, then check your
answers using the grid opposite.

**4**　　**7**　　**6**　　**3**　　**9**

**5**

**2**　　**8**　　**5**　　**1**

Now fill in these gaps:

9 + [　] = 10

[　] + 7 = 10

5 + [　] = 10

[　] + 4 = 10

8 + [　] = 10

ALWAYS PLAY SPOT THE BOND!

25

NUMBER BONDS

# ADDING NUMBER BONDS

Pirate Blacktooth has five bags of coins.
Each bag must contain ten coins. If they don't, draw them in.

Now he is weighing his bags of coins. Each batch must add up to 10. Write in the number of coins the second bag should have.

8 [ ] 10

6 [ ] 10

3 [ ] 10

26

# PIRATE BLACKTOOTH'S SHIVERING EQUATIONS

Do these equations as quickly as possible.

Arr! You've passed your first pirate lesson.

$7 + \boxed{\phantom{0}} = 10$

$\boxed{\phantom{0}} + 5 = 10$

$2 + \boxed{\phantom{0}} = 10$

$9 + \boxed{\phantom{0}} = 10$

$\boxed{\phantom{0}} + 3 = 10$

$5 + \boxed{\phantom{0}} = 10$

$1 + \boxed{\phantom{0}} = 10$

$\boxed{\phantom{0}} + 4 = 10$

$6 + \boxed{\phantom{0}} = 10$

$8 + \boxed{\phantom{0}} = 10$

READY FOR MORE PIRATE PRACTICE?

27

# SUBTRACTING NUMBER BONDS

Pirate Blacktooth has to buy provisions for his journey. Here are his bags of 10 coins. If he buys each item, how many coins will he have left in each bag?

**3 COINS**

$10 - 3 = \boxed{\phantom{0}}$

**8 COINS**

$10 - 8 = \boxed{\phantom{0}}$

**5 COINS**

$10 - 5 = \boxed{\phantom{0}}$

**4 COINS**

$10 - 4 = \boxed{\phantom{0}}$

**9 COINS**

$10 - 9 = \boxed{\phantom{0}}$

# PIRATE BLACKTOOTH'S SUBTRACTION EQUATIONS

Try doing these as quickly as possible.

10 - 2 = ☐

10 - ☐ = 5

10 - 3 = ☐

10 - 8 = ☐

10 - ☐ = 3

10 - 9 = ☐

10 - ☐ = 2

10 - 4 = ☐

10 - 5 = ☐

10 - ☐ = 9

Shiver me timbers! You've passed your second pirate lesson.

NOW FOR SOME PIRATE PUZZLES.

29

# PIRATE BLACKTOOTH'S BRAIN-TEASERS

Pirate Blacktooth has found lots of gold coins. He adds them up using number bonds. Do the same, crossing out the coins as you go. Keep count of the number of bonds on your fingers or in your head.

| 1 | 8 | 2 | 5 | 5 |
|---|---|---|---|---|
| 6 | 7 | 9 | 1 | 4 |
| 7 | 9 | 3 | 2 | 6 |
| 3 | 7 | 5 | 4 | 8 |
| 9 | 1 | 2 | 3 | 8 |

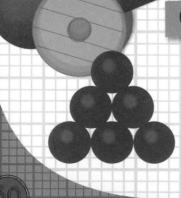

How many tens does he have? ☐

One coin is left over. What is its value? ☐

If Blacktooth has **6** cannonballs, how many does he buy to make **10**? ☐

If he then fires **3** at Pirate Bonny's ship, how many does he have left? ☐

Can you balance these bags of coins?

5 + [ ] = 10

9 + [ ] = 10

Blacktooth is doing what he likes best—piling up his jewels. How many must he add to each pile to make three piles of ten?

6 + [ ]    9 + [ ]    7 + [ ]

Try these equations:

[ ] - 3 = 7

10 - 2 = [ ]

10 - 1 = [ ]

Aye, aye! You've passed pirate lesson number three!

YOU'RE GETTING GOOD AT NUMBER BONDS.

# DOUBLE TROUBLE

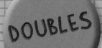

Learning doubles is another way of making addition easier. Here they are:

1 + 1 = 2

2 + 2 = 4

3 + 3 = 6

4 + 4 = 8

5 + 5 = 10

6 + 6 = 12

7 + 7 = 14

8 + 8 = 16

9 + 9 = 18

10 + 10 = 20

Now cover up the answers. Can you remember them?

# LEARNING WITH PARROT PETE

DOUBLES

Parrot Pete is a doubling expert. If he's good, Blacktooth doubles the number of peanuts he gives him. Here's what Blacktooth gives Pete on Monday.

$$5 + 5 = \boxed{10}$$

On Tuesday, Blacktooth gives Pete one extra for being REALLY good. Since this is almost double, Pete can simply add one more.

$$5 + 6 = \boxed{\phantom{00}}$$

On Wednesday, Blacktooth doesn't have quite enough peanuts to double the number. He's one short, so how many does Pete get?

$$5 + 4 = \boxed{\phantom{00}}$$

READY TO DO THE OPPOSITE?

# HALF MEASURES

Halving is the INVERSE of doubling, which means it is the opposite action. Can you halve these numbers by splitting them into equal numbers?

4 = 2 + 2

20 = ◯ + ◯

12 = ◯ + ◯

10 = ◯ + ◯

6 = ◯ + ◯

16 = ◯ + ◯

8 = ◯ + ◯

14 = ◯ + ◯

2 = ◯ + ◯

18 = ◯ + ◯

Check your answers by adding them together.

# LEARNING WITH PARROT PETE

I love counting seeds!

When Pete is naughty, Blacktooth halves the number of seeds he gives him. On Thursday, Blacktooth was going to give Pete six seeds, but he only gives him half.

6 - 3 = **3**

On Friday, Pete is REALLY naughty, so Blacktooth takes away one more. Since this is almost half, Pete can calculate this by simply taking one away from half.

6 - 4 =

READY FOR SOME PRACTICE?

35

# PARROT PETE'S PARROT PRACTICE

Pete needs help with these equations. They are either doubles or almost doubles.

Who's a clever kid, then?

$8 + 8 = \boxed{\phantom{00}}$

$8 + 7 = \boxed{\phantom{00}}$

$10 + 10 = \boxed{\phantom{00}}$

$10 + \boxed{\phantom{00}} = 21$

$\boxed{\phantom{00}} + 3 = 6$

$3 + 4 = \boxed{\phantom{00}}$

$\boxed{\phantom{00}} + 5 = 10$

$6 + \boxed{\phantom{00}} = 11$

$7 + 7 = \boxed{\phantom{00}}$

$6 + 7 = \boxed{\phantom{00}}$

$12 = 6 + \boxed{\phantom{0}}$

$13 = 6 + \boxed{\phantom{0}}$

Now help him with these ones. They are either halves or almost halves. Can you fill in the missing numbers?

$2 = 1 + \boxed{\phantom{0}}$

$3 = 1 + \boxed{\phantom{0}}$

$10 = 5 + \boxed{\phantom{0}}$

$9 = 5 + \boxed{\phantom{0}}$

$4 = 2 + \boxed{\phantom{0}}$

$5 = 2 + \boxed{\phantom{0}}$

$8 = 4 + \boxed{\phantom{0}}$

$7 = 4 + \boxed{\phantom{0}}$

If you got the last one right, can you do this one?

$80 = 40 + \boxed{\phantom{0}}$

$70 = 40 + \boxed{\phantom{0}}$

NOW TEST YOURSELF WITH SOME FUN PUZZLES.

# PARROT PETE'S BRAIN-TEASERS

If you get stuck, go back to page 32!

Parrot Pete is **6** years old. The ship's cat is double his age. How old is she?

Pete cost Blacktooth **16** gold coins. The other parrots cost half that amount. How much did they cost?

It takes **8** seconds for Pete to fly to the crow's nest. How long does it take him to fly there and back?

seconds

If double **9** is **18**, what is **9 + 10**?

If half a pizza has **3** slices, how many does a whole pizza have?

Parrot Pete wouldn't come when Pirate Blacktooth called! Blacktooth was going to give him **10** peanuts and **20** seeds, but Blacktooth halves that amount. How many of each does Pete get?

Peanuts          Seeds

YOU'RE A SHIPSHAPE PIRATE'S MATE.

# REMEMBER IT!

Can you remember your number bonds? Here are some equations to refresh your memory.

$$10 - \boxed{\phantom{00}} = 8$$

$$4 + \boxed{\phantom{00}} = 10$$

$$3 + \boxed{\phantom{00}} = 10$$

$$10 - 1 = \boxed{\phantom{00}}$$

$$10 - 5 = \boxed{\phantom{00}}$$

Which two numbers do not add up to 10?

5 and 5          1 and 8          3 and 7

9 and 1          6 and 4

Pirate Blacktooth is back to weighing coins. Write in the number that will balance the bags.

2    [ ]    10

That's great, shipmate!

Now let's test your halving and doubling.

Blacktooth has **20** diamonds, **18** rubies, **8** sapphires, and **14** emeralds in his treasure chest. His arch rival, Pirate Bonny, steals half of each. How many does he have left?

Diamonds ◯

Sapphires ◯

Rubies ◯

Emeralds ◯

It takes Parrot Pete **3** hours to fly from one island to the next. How many hours does it take him to fly there and back? ◯

If **10 + 10 = 20**, what is **11 + 10**? ◯

ARR ... YOU'RE AN ADDING STAR.

41

# TENS AND UNITS

Bella Butterfly is an expert at tens and units. She has to be—she has **6** dots on the left wing and **6** on the right. Add them together, and they make **12**!

$$6 \quad + \quad 6 \quad = 12$$

To make counting easy, we group every set of **10** together, and the units are what's left over.

$$6 \quad + \quad 6 \quad = 10 + 2$$

So there is one set of 10, with 2 units left over. This is shown below, with a tens column and a units column.

| TENS | UNITS |
|------|-------|
| 1    | 2     |

This makes **12**.

# TIME FOR PRACTICE

Bella has made a test for you. For the groups below, write how many tens and units there are.

| TENS | UNITS |
|------|-------|
| ◯    | ◯     |

| TENS | UNITS |
|------|-------|
| ◯    | ◯     |

| TENS | UNITS |
|------|-------|
| ◯    | ◯     |

Now try these.
In each of the numbers, circle the tens.

24   95   73   55   68   17

Now circle the units.

65   84   24   66   57   48

Excellent!

READY FOR SOME MORE PRACTICE?

# TIME TO ADD TENS

When adding 10 to any number, you don't need to count on every time. You just need to add another group of 10 to the tens column. Try these equations.

23 + 10 = ◯

42 + 10 = ◯

10 + 57 = ◯

10 + 51 = ◯

64 + 10 = ◯

43 + 10 = ◯

Remember, when adding 10, the units stay the same.

# TIME TO SUBTRACT TENS

When subtracting 10 from any number, you don't need to count back. You just take away a group of 10 from the tens column. Try these equations.

Good luck!

67 - 10 =

18 - 10 =

21 - 10 =

33 - 10 =

49 - 10 =

82 - 10 =

READY FOR SOME PUZZLES?

When subtracting 10, the units also stay the same.

45

# BELLA BUTTERFLY'S
# BRAIN-TEASERS

Good luck!

Bella Butterfly has collected **35** petals. She collects **10** more. How many does she have?

What is the total of **20** and **10**?

Which of these numbers is the same as five tens and six units?

56        65        5106        506

Bella's friend Colin Caterpillar comes to stay for a week, then he stays another 10 days. How many days does he stay in total?

At the bug ball, there are **23** butterflies, **10** grasshoppers, and **10** caterpillars.

How many bugs are there in total?

If the grasshoppers leave, how many bugs are left?

If the caterpillars leave as well, how many bugs are left?

If all the caterpillars and grasshoppers go to buy a lollipop each, how many lollipops do they buy?

GREAT ADDING AND TAKING AWAY!

**Try these ones!**

# TENS AND HUNDREDS

Hattie Hen is the egg-laying queen of her farm. She lays **10** eggs a week. Here's the farmer's record. Can you fill in the missing totals?

| Week | Eggs | Total |
|------|------|-------|
| 1 | 10 | 10 |
| 2 | 10 | 20 |
| 3 | 10 | |
| 4 | 10 | 40 |
| 5 | 10 | |
| 6 | 10 | 60 |
| 7 | 10 | |
| 8 | 10 | 80 |
| 9 | 10 | |
| 10 | 10 | 100 |

When a group of ten is added to 90, you get 10 tens, which is 100 (a triple-digit number).

# WHAT ARE HUNDREDS?

The number **100** can be written with a hundreds column, a tens column, and a units column. It is one group of a hundred, with no tens and no units.

| HUNDREDS | TENS | UNITS |
|----------|------|-------|
| 1 | 0 | 0 |

Remember 10 tens make a hundred.

See what happens if you add **10** to **100**.

| HUNDREDS | TENS | UNITS |
|----------|------|-------|
| 1 | 1 | 0 |

So ... $100 + 10 = 110$

Look what happens if you add **90** to **110**. Write in the answer below.

| HUNDREDS | TENS | UNITS |
|----------|------|-------|
| 2 | 0 | 0 |

So ... $110 + 90 =$ 

NOW FOR SOME PRACTICE.

49

# TIME TO ADD 10s AND 100s

Help Hattie Hen with these equations.

$110 + 50 =$ H T U ⬭⬭⬭

$200 + 200 =$ H T U ⬭⬭⬭

$110 + 10 =$ H T U ⬭⬭⬭

$160 + 30 =$ H T U ⬭⬭⬭

Cock-a-doodle-doo! Here's more to do.

$210 + 70 =$ ⬭

$120 + 60 =$ ⬭

$300 + 40 =$ ⬭

Try this one, if you're feeling clucky ...

$190 + 20 =$ ⬭

Hattie is now trying to subtract 100s and 10s.
Can you help with these equations?

120 - 20 = H T U ◯ ◯ ◯

650 - 200 = H T U ◯ ◯ ◯

270 - 50 = H T U ◯ ◯ ◯

150 - 40 = H T U ◯ ◯ ◯

What about these ones?

340 - 30 = ◯

20 - 20 = ◯

Finding them hard? Don't fret. Just look at the end!

Try this one, if you're feeling plucky ...

330 - 110 = ◯

GREAT EFFORT. GOOD JOB!

# HATTIE HEN'S BRAIN-TEASERS

After four weeks, Hattie has laid **40** eggs. The farmer gives **20** to his mother and **10** to his brother. How many does he have left?

The farmer has containers that can store **10** eggs each.

He packs **5** containers. How many eggs are inside?

If he gives away **2** containers, how many eggs does he have left?

What is the total of three tens and three tens?

Which of these numbers is the same as three hundreds and five tens?

315      35      3005      350      530

What is 80 plus 100 plus 10?

Circle the equation that has a different answer to the rest.

80 - 30        70 - 30        40 + 10

100 - 50        30 + 20        90 - 40

Cluck-cluck! Check the answer if you're stuck.

EGG-CELLENT JOB!

# NUMBER BONDS TO 20

All good pirates know the numbers that make up 10, but really smart pirates know them up to 20! Here they are. Look at them, learn them, cover them up, and remember them.

$$11 + 9 = 20$$
$$12 + 8 = 20$$
$$13 + 7 = 20$$
$$14 + 6 = 20$$
$$15 + 5 = 20$$
$$16 + 4 = 20$$
$$17 + 3 = 20$$
$$18 + 2 = 20$$
$$19 + 1 = 20$$

Can you see the difference between number bonds to 10 and to 20? See page 24.

# LEARNING NUMBER BONDS

Spotting number bonds makes equations easier.

If you look at the units, you'll see that they are the same as the number bonds that make 10. That's because $11 + 9$ is the same as $10 + 1 + 9$, which is two tens. Here's this equation written in columns.

| TENS | UNITS |
|------|-------|
| 1    | 1     |
|      | 9 +   |
|------|-------|
| 2    | 0     |

Can you circle the equation that does not add up to 20?

19 + 1

13 + 7

2 + 18

5 + 15

6 + 13

I SPY A CLEVER PIRATE.

55

# FIND THE NUMBER BONDS TO 20

Pirate Bonny is Blacktooth's arch enemy. She is hoping to outwit him with her quick mathematics skills. Can you help?

$17 +$ ☐ $= 20$

☐ $+ 4 = 20$

$1 +$ ☐ $= 20$

☐ $+ 15 = 20$

$18 +$ ☐ $= 20$

Now try this equation.

$22 + 8 =$ ☐

A pirate salute to you, if you got the last one right.

# PIRATE BONNY'S BRAINY EQUATIONS

Now, me hearties, try to solve this little bunch.

$20 - \boxed{\phantom{0}} = 14$

$20 - \boxed{\phantom{0}} = 13$

$20 - \boxed{\phantom{0}} = 11$

$20 - \boxed{\phantom{0}} = 12$

$20 - \boxed{\phantom{0}} = 10$

Circle the two numbers whose total does not add up to **20**.

11 AND 8

6 AND 14

15 AND 5

18 AND 2

13 AND 7

GET TO KNOW YOUR NUMBER BONDS.

57

# WHAT'S THE DIFFERENCE?

If you are asked the difference between one great white shark and three little fish, what would you say? Size? Teeth? One eats the other? Well, in mathematics, the right answer is ... 2!

**1 SHARK**

**3 FISH**

The difference between 6 fish and 2 fish is a hungry tummy!

In mathematics, the question really is, what is the **difference in number**? If there are 3 fish and 1 shark, the difference in number is 2.

The difference between **6** fish and **2** fish is **4** fish. You can see it on this number line.

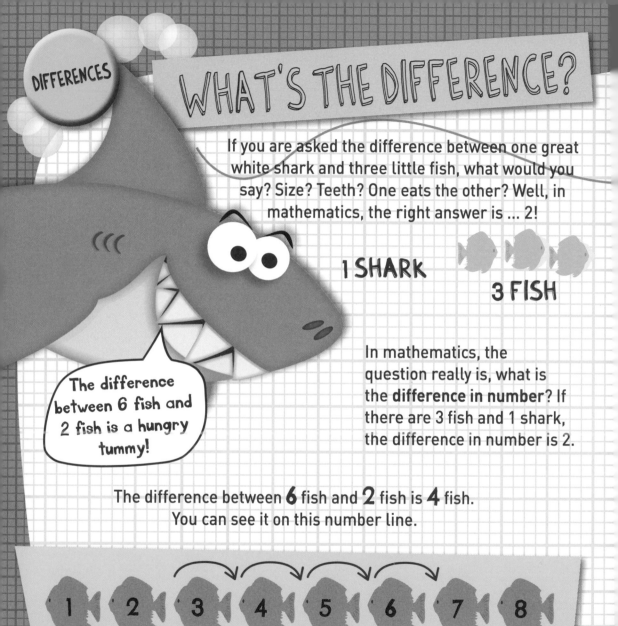

| 1 | 2 | 3 | 4 | 5 | 6 | 7 | 8 |

4

# FINDING THE DIFFERENCE

There are many ways to find the difference between two numbers. To find the difference between **20** and **17**, you could count on.

| 15 | 16 | 17 | 18 | 19 | 20 | 21 | 22 |

You could also count back.

| 15 | 16 | 17 | 18 | 19 | 20 | 21 | 22 |

You could write the equation down.

$$20 - 17 =$$

Or you could do the equation in your head. (Remember your number bonds?)

Whichever way you choose, the answer is the same. Write it here.

COOL CALCULATING!

# SID'S EQUATION SOLVING

Sid Shark has spied two groups of fish.
What is the difference between the two?

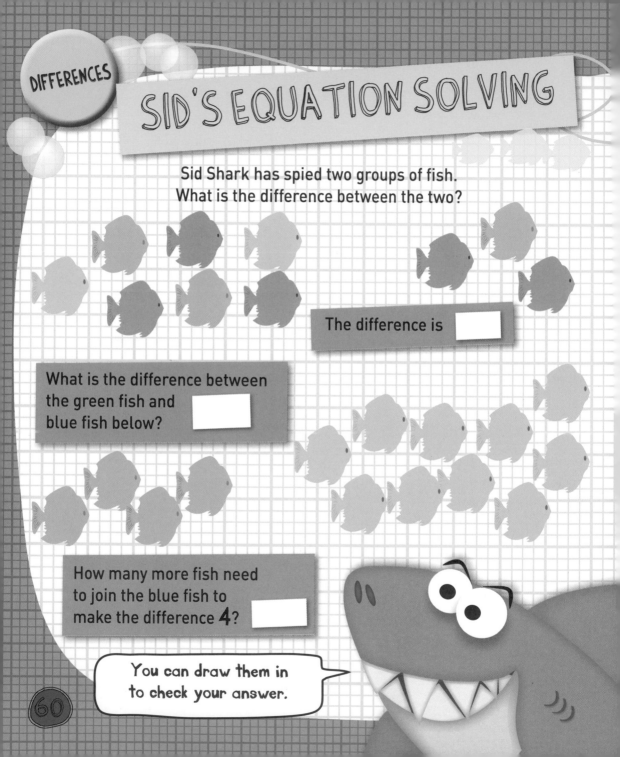

The difference is [ ]

What is the difference between the green fish and blue fish below? [ ]

How many more fish need to join the blue fish to make the difference **4**? [ ]

You can draw them in to check your answer.

DIFFERENCES

How many of these pairs of bubbles have a difference of 5? ▢

1 6    9 4    19 13    11 6    7 2    12 5

By calculating the differences between the numbers, can you finish these sequences?

1   3   5   7   ▢

16   13   10   7   ▢

6   7   9   12   ▢

Now find the differences between these numbers.

14 AND 17   ▢

18 AND 6   ▢

2 AND 9   ▢

NOW IT'S TEST TIME.

# SID SHARK'S
## BRAIN-TEASERS

Sid has visited **2** islands. His dad has been to **4**. What's the difference between the two?

ISLANDS

When Sid was younger, he had **32** teeth. Now he has **40** teeth. Find the difference.

Sid is sharing out his shell collection between his three brothers.

A

B

C

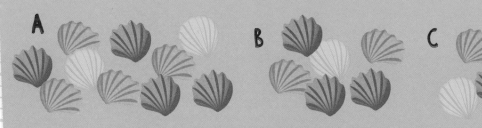

How many does he need to add to **B** and **C** to make all three piles the same?

B

C

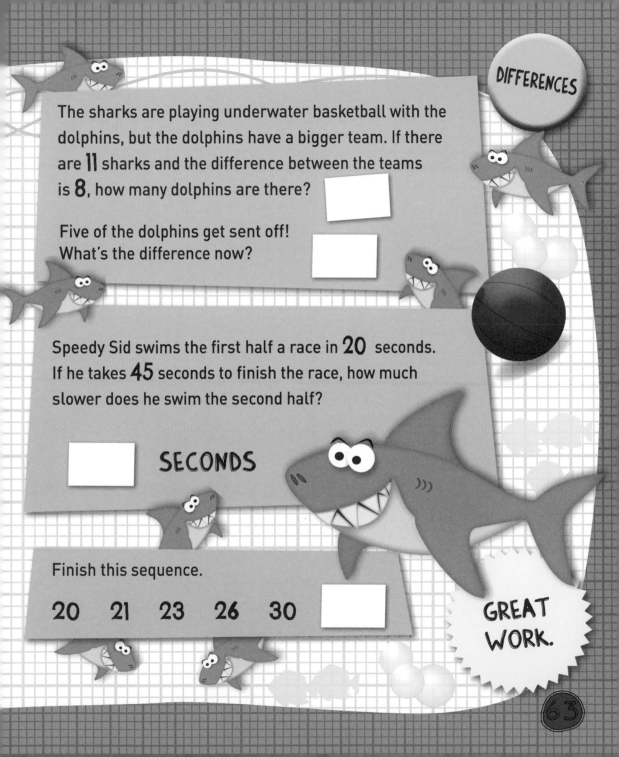

The sharks are playing underwater basketball with the dolphins, but the dolphins have a bigger team. If there are 11 sharks and the difference between the teams is 8, how many dolphins are there?

Five of the dolphins get sent off! What's the difference now?

Speedy Sid swims the first half a race in 20 seconds. If he takes 45 seconds to finish the race, how much slower does he swim the second half?

SECONDS

GREAT WORK.

Finish this sequence.

20  21  23  26  30

63

# REMEMBER IT!

It's time to see if you can remember all about 10s and 100s, number bonds and differences.

If Whiz-Bang has **10** green bottles and **5** purple bottles, what is the difference?

Pirate Bonny is weighing her gold. On one side, she has **20** coins, and on the other, she has **50**. Circle the number that will balance the scales.

20    50

**10**

**20**

**30**

Last week, Hattie Hen laid **7** eggs. This week she laid **10**. What's the difference?

Sid Shark joins a swimathon with his friends.

Sid does **40** laps to the island and back.

Chuckles does **30** laps

Little Blue does **20** laps.

How many laps do they do in total?

Find the number bonds!

Circle the two numbers whose answer would not end in 0 (zero).

| 41 | 8 |

| 22 | 8 |     | 6 | 34 |

| 55 | 5 |     | 63 | 7 |

TOP NUMBER WIZARD!

# ADDING DOUBLE DIGITS

When you add double digits that have both tens and units, the easiest way is to add the tens first and then the units.

$$17 + 12 = 10 + 10 = 20 \text{ (2 tens)}$$
$$7 + 2 = 9 \text{ (9 units)}$$

Then add the two answers together.
$$17 + 12 = 20 + 9 = 29$$

Can you do this one?

$$11 + 13 = 10 + 10 = \boxed{\phantom{00}}$$
$$1 + 3 = \boxed{\phantom{00}}$$

Add the answers together.

$$11 + 13 = \boxed{\phantom{00}} + \boxed{\phantom{00}} = \boxed{\phantom{00}}$$

When you add double digits, sometimes the units add up to 10 or more than 10. See what happens.

$$17 + 13 = 10 + 10 = 20 \text{ (2 tens)}$$
$$7 + 3 = 10 \text{ (1 ten)}$$

So there are 3 tens and 0 units.   $17 + 13 = 20 + 10 = 30$

There is another way to add tricky double-digit equations. It's called "rounding up," and it's useful when one or both of the numbers are near tens, such as $19 + 19$.

You already know that $20 + 20 = 40$.

You know that $19$ is one less than $20$.
So if you round up the equation by one, you can calculate easily—you simply take away the units that you added from the answer.

Here's how it works:

$19 + 1 + 19 + 1$ is the same as $20 + 20$.

So, $19 + 19 = 40 - 1 - 1 = 38$

Can you do this one?

$29 + 19 = \boxed{\phantom{00}}$

READY FOR SOME PRACTICE?

# ZEE THE ZEBRA'S EQUATIONS

Try doing the equations in your head.

Zee the Zebra has come up with these equations for you. First add the tens, then the units, and add the answers together.

24 + 15 = ☐

82 + 16 = ☐

18 + 11 = ☐

23 + 23 = ☐

31 + 24 = ☐

55 + 14 = ☐

57 + 22 = ☐

21 + 42 = ☐

66 + 33 = ☐

Now try this one.

79 + 11 = ☐

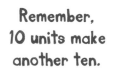

Remember, 10 units make another ten.

$29 + 29 = \boxed{\phantom{000}}$

$39 + 19 = \boxed{\phantom{000}}$

$49 + 39 = \boxed{\phantom{000}}$

$109 + 29 = \boxed{\phantom{000}}$

$59 + 19 = \boxed{\phantom{000}}$

$19 + 69 = \boxed{\phantom{000}}$

$79 + 19 = \boxed{\phantom{000}}$

$49 + 49 = \boxed{\phantom{000}}$

$29 + 49 = \boxed{\phantom{000}}$

If you round up by 1, you take away 1 from the answer. If you round up by 2, you take away 2!

Now try this one.

$19 + 18 = \boxed{\phantom{000}}$

ZIPPETY ZEBRAS, YOU'RE GETTING GOOD!

69

# SUBTRACTING DOUBLE DIGITS

You still ADD the answers.

You can use the same method of subtracting the tens and units when subtracting double digits—but ONLY if both digits of the first number are BIGGER than those in the second number.

$36 - 12 = 30 - 10 = 20$ (2 tens)

$6 - 2 = 4$ (4 units)

Then add the two answers together.

$36 - 12 = 20 + 4 = 24$

Can you do this one?

$26 - 15 = 20 - 10 =$ ▢

$6 - 5 =$ ▢

Add the answers together.

$26 - 15 =$ ▢ $+$ ▢ $=$ ▢

70

# ROUNDING UP AND DOWN

You can also use rounding with subtraction. Here's a tricky equation.

$$90 - 19 =$$

With subtracting, when you round UP, you ADD to the answer. When you round down, you TAKE AWAY.

You already know that $90 - 20 = 70$.

As **19** is one less than **20**, you are taking away one less from **90**, so your answer will be one more.

$$90 - 19 = 70 + 1 = 71$$

With subtraction, rounding down can also be helpful. Here's another equation.

$$90 - 21 =$$

Since **21** is one more than **20**, you are taking away one more from **90**, so your answer will be one less.

$$90 - 21 = 70 - 1 = \boxed{\phantom{00}}$$

READY FOR SOME PRACTICE?

DOUBLE DIGITS

# GEORGIE GIRAFFE TAKES AWAY

On the other side of the plain, Georgie Giraffe is struggling with her own equations. Can you help her by subtracting the tens and then the units?

36 – 25 =

28 – 11 =

67 – 31 =

32 – 12 =

54 – 22 =

97 – 86 =

79 – 52 =

21 – 10 =

44 – 13 =

85 – 23 =

Try doing the equations in your head.

Don't forget, 100 is the same as 10 tens.

Now try this one.

101 – 91 =

# GEORGIE'S ROUNDING UP

**DOUBLE DIGITS**

## ROUNDING UP EQUATIONS

Since you are rounding up, ADD 1 to the answer.

70 - 19 =

60 - 29 =

30 - 19 =

100 - 89 =

## ROUNDING DOWN EQUATIONS

Since you are rounding down, you TAKE AWAY 1 from the answer.

80 - 21 =

50 - 31 =

40 - 11 =

100 - 11 =

JUMPING GIRAFFES. YOU ARE GETTING IT!

73

# GEORGIE'S NUMBER LINES

Georgie Giraffe also uses number lines and differences to do REALLY tricky equations.

$$73 - 54 =$$

Here's how she does it.

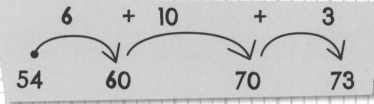

Counting on from **54** to **60** is easy. The answer is **6**.

The difference between **60** and **70** is **10**.

From **70** to **73**, you count on **3**.

So breaking down the equation on a number line into easy chunks makes a difficult equation much easier. The difference

between **73** and **54** is ... **6 + 10 + 3 = 19**

Calculate the answer to the equations, using the number lines.

92 - 75 = ☐

5 + 10 + 2

75    80    90    92

81 - 38 = ☐

See if you can do the next equations, putting your own numbers on the number line.

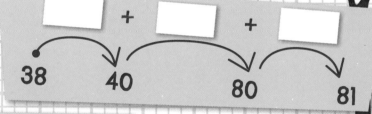

☐ + ☐ + ☐

38    40    80    81

74 - 57 = ☐

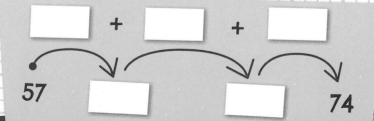

☐ + ☐ + ☐

57    ☐    ☐    74

TRICKY JUST GOT EASY! GOOD JOB.

# ZEE AND GEORGIE'S BRAIN-TEASERS

Zee and Georgie are at the watering hole. Zee has taken **34** sips, and Georgie has taken **35**. How many have they taken in total?

Who's been walking in the mud?

Georgie leaves **30** footprints.

Zee leaves **19** footprints.

What is the difference?

Georgie eats **100** leaves a day in the winter and **65** leaves a day in the summer. How many fewer does she eat in the summer?

There are **75** zebras in Zee's herd. **54** are female. How many are male?

Of the **75** zebras, **10** are babies and another **15** are young ones. How many is that in total?

So, if the rest are adults, how many are there?

It's the night of the Great Plains Quiz. Each correct answer scores 2 points.

The zebras have **34** points.
The giraffes have **22** points.
The smarty-pants elephants have **58** points.

By how many points are the elephants beating:

The zebras?          The giraffes?

Are the elephants beating both teams put together?     YES     NO

THAT'S WILD!

# ADDING BIG AND LONG EQUATIONS

This is Professor Chipmunk. He has built a magnificent number machine. He can put in any number or any number of numbers, and it will add them up for him.

He puts in these supersized equations:

45 + 320 + 210 =          902 + 72 + 13 =

| 45 | 210 |
|----|-----|
| | 320 |

| 72 | 13 |
|----|-----|
| | 902 |

| H | T | U |
|---|---|---|
| 3 | 2 | 0 |
| 2 | 1 | 0 |
| | 4 | 5 |

ADD

HUNDREDS 5

TENS 7

UNITS 5

TOTAL 5 7 5

| H | T | U |
|---|---|---|
| 9 | 0 | 2 |
| | 7 | 2 |
| | 1 | 3 |

ADD

HUNDREDS 9

TENS 8

UNITS 7

TOTAL 9 8 7

# THE MAGNIFICENT NUMBER MACHINE

Can you fill in the answer windows, based on the numbers going into the machine at the top?

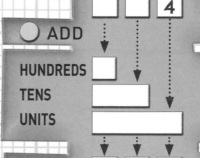

| 22 | 4 |
| --- | --- |
| | 720 |

| H | T | U |
| --- | --- | --- |
| 7 | 2 2 | 0 2 4 |

○ ADD

HUNDREDS

TENS

UNITS

TOTAL

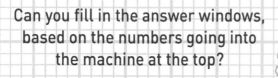

| 73 | 23 |
| --- | --- |
| | 203 |

| H | T | U |
| --- | --- | --- |
| 2 | 7 2 0 | 3 3 3 |

○ ADD

HUNDREDS

TENS

UNITS

TOTAL

OUTSTANDING!

# THE PROFESSOR'S PRACTICE

Can you calculate these supersized equations using the magnificent number machine?

12 + 560 + 215 =
702 + 31 + 124 =

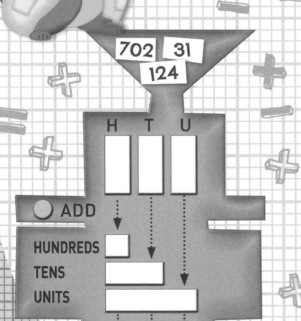

| 12 | 560 |
| --- | --- |
| 215 | |

H   T   U

○ ADD

HUNDREDS
TENS
UNITS

TOTAL

| 702 | 31 |
| --- | --- |
| 124 | |

H   T   U

○ ADD

HUNDREDS
TENS
UNITS

TOTAL

Now try this
one without
the machine.

653 +
33 +
12 =

Write your
answer here. →

80

# AWESOME BIG EQUATIONS

Try this equation:

$$201 + 53 + 102 =$$

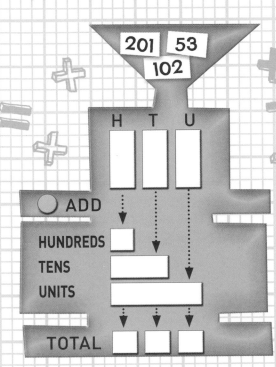

Now try these four without the machine.

Write your answers here. →

$$317 + 60 + 2 =$$
_____
_____

$$466 + 12 + 1 =$$
_____
_____

$$555 + 31 + 100 =$$
_____
_____

$$805 + 23 + 20 =$$
_____
_____

MAGNIFICENT!

81

# REMEMBER IT!

Are adding and subtracting double and triple digits really easy now? Let's see how you get on with this little recap.

65 + 12 = ☐

72 - 61 = ☐

70 + 22 = ☐

55 + 25 = ☐

87 - 64 = ☐

33 + 33 = ☐

69 + 69 = ☐

59 + 49 = ☐

109 + 29 = ☐

Use rounding for the equations above and below.

30 - 21 = ☐

90 - 39 = ☐

100 - 51 = ☐

If Georgie collects **62** ostrich feathers and Zee collects **37**, how many do they have in total? ☐

Using the number line below, can you do this hard equation?

62 − 47 = ☐

47     50          60        62

Use Professor Chipmunk's magnificent number machine to do this equation:

212 + 121 + 221 =

Now try this one without the machine.

207 +
602 +
  80 =
_____
_____

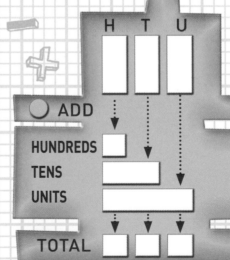

212   121
   221

H   T   U

◯ ADD

HUNDREDS
TENS
UNITS

TOTAL

# MONEY MATTERS

Cool Dog sells ice cream to dogs at the park. He has to be quick at adding up and giving change! Here's his price list in Doggy Dollars and Canine Cents.

| COOL CONE | TASTY CONE | T-BONE | YUMMY CUP |
|:---:|:---:|:---:|:---:|
| 15¢ | 20¢ | 25¢ | 25¢ |

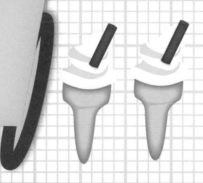

His first customers ask for two Tasty Cones. In his head, Cool Dog adds it up:

$$20¢ + 20¢ = 40¢$$

They give him $1.

Knowing that $1 is the same as 100¢, Cool Dog calculates how much change to give them: 100¢ − 40¢ = 60¢

His next customers ask for a Cool Cone and a T-Bone.
Cool Dog calculates what to charge them.

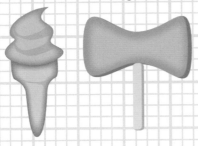

They give him **50¢**. What change
should he give them?

50¢ - 40¢ = [ ]

15¢ + 25¢ = 40¢

More customers
want two Cool
Cones and
a Yummy Cup.
What should Cool
Dog charge them
for the three ice
creams?

15¢ + 15¢ + 25¢ = [ ]

They give him **60¢**.
What change should he give them? [ ]

READY
FOR SOME
PRACTICE?

85

# COOL DOG'S MONEY PRACTICE

You can use a piece of paper to calculate the equations.

Here is Cool Dog's price list again.

| COOL CONE | TASTY CONE | T-BONE | YUMMY CUP |
|-----------|------------|--------|-----------|
| 15¢ | 20¢ | 25¢ | 25¢ |

Below is a shopping list with the money the customer has to pay with. Cool Dog adds up the total and calculates the change. Can you do the same for the two lists on the next page?

**50¢**

| | COST |
|---|---|
| 2 COOL CONES | 30¢ |
| TASTY CONE | 20¢ |
| TOTAL | 50¢ |
| CHANGE | 0 |

# COOL DOG'S CALCULATIONS

**$1** **50¢** COST

2 COOL CONES
2 TASTY CONES
1 YUMMY CUP
1 T-BONE

TOTAL CHANGE

**$1** COST

1 T-BONE
1 YUMMY CUP

TOTAL CHANGE

If you have **$1**, what is the maximum number of ice creams you can buy?

Which ice cream would you buy?

GOOD WORK!

87

# MONEY

# COOL DOG'S BRAIN-TEASERS

If one Cool Cone is **15¢** and one Yummy Cup is **25¢**, how much is that in total?

At the end of the afternoon, Cool Dog has taken **$5.10**. Yesterday, he took **$6.20**.
What's the difference?

A customer comes with **50¢** and needs **3** ice creams.
She has two options. How much change does she get with each?

## OPTION 1

CHANGE

15¢  15¢  15¢

## OPTION 2

CHANGE

15¢  15¢  20¢

You have these coins in your pocket. How much do they add up to?

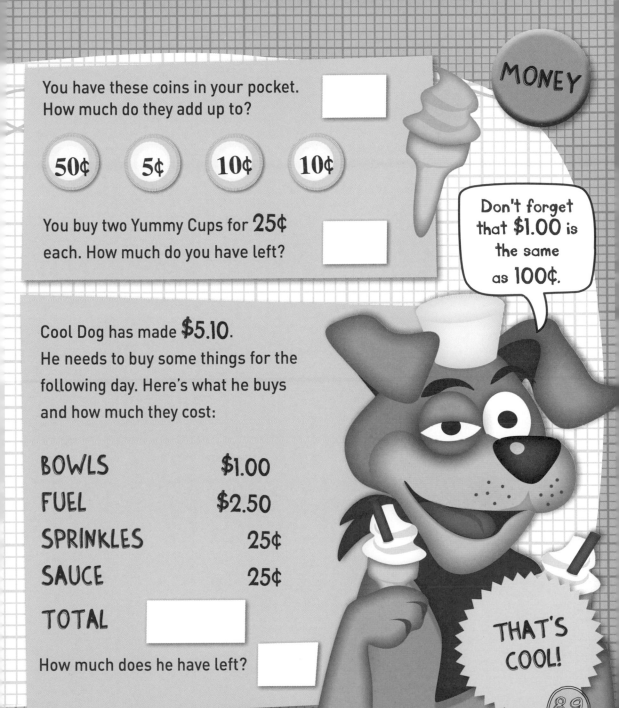

50¢  5¢  10¢  10¢

You buy two Yummy Cups for **25¢** each. How much do you have left?

MONEY

Don't forget that $1.00 is the same as 100¢.

Cool Dog has made **$5.10**.
He needs to buy some things for the following day. Here's what he buys and how much they cost:

| | |
|---|---|
| BOWLS | $1.00 |
| FUEL | $2.50 |
| SPRINKLES | 25¢ |
| SAUCE | 25¢ |
| TOTAL | |

How much does he have left?

THAT'S COOL!

# THE ULTIMATE TEST

Are you ready to test yourself using all the techniques you've learned in this book? If you write your answers on a piece of paper, you can test yourself again. Ready?

Remember ... count on, count back, and number bonds.

3 + 6 = ☐    9 + 2 = ☐

10 + 7 = ☐    5 + 5 = ☐

Circle the term that has nothing to do with subtraction.

TAKE AWAY   MINUS   DECREASE   TIMES   DIFFERENCE

Can you halve **20**? ☐    Can you double **8**? ☐

60 - 20 = ☐    20 + 10 = ☐    10 + 35 = ☐

What's the difference between **10** and **15**? ☐

Balance these bags of coins.

8    ☐    10

78 + 11 = ☐    100 - 80 = ☐    68 + 2 = ☐

65 - 35 = ☐    92 - 71 = ☐    44 - 13 = ☐

If you have **75¢**, and the ice creams are **20¢** each,
how many can you buy? ☐
How much change would you get? ☐

Remember ten units makes a ten.

How many pairs of bubbles have a difference of **8**.

22  20  58  5
14  12  50  13

☐

Thinking about the magical number machine, can you do this equation?

$$240 +$$
$$34 +$$
$$\underline{202 =}$$
$$\underline{\phantom{000}}$$

Use the number line to do this tricky sum.

103 - 77 = ☐

77  ☐   ☐   103

Now check your answers. Are you an amazing
mathematics magician or still a sorcerer's apprentice?

# WHIZ-BANG'S ANSWERS

Page 5
43 - 9 = 34

Page 6
37 + 3 = 40

Page 8
2 + 1 = 3
3 + 1 = 4
4 + 1 = 5
5 + 1 = 6
6 + 1 = 7
7 + 1 = 8
Merlin needs to make
2 more trips.

Page 9
13 + 1 = 14
10 + 1 = 11
25 + 1 = 26
31 + 1 = 32
3 + 1 = 4
59 + 1 = 60
99 + 1 = 100
199 + 1 = 200
222 + 1 = 223

Page 10
4 + 3 = 7
0 + 2 = 2
4 + 4 = 8
8 + 4 = 12
5 + 1 = 6

Merlin has 8 brothers and
8 sisters. That's 16 in total.

Page 11
6 + 4 = 10
10 + 6 = 16
16 + 3 = 19
5 + 0 = 5
21 + 9 = 30
52 + 2 = 54
48 + 2 = 50

5 + 53 = 58
1 + 101 = 102
8 + 35 = 43

Page 12
Merlin is playing with
8 brothers.
He has 7 chunks of cheese.
PRODUCT does not mean
add (it means multiply).

Page 13
Merlin will be 6.
Mudge has won with
12 points. Merlin has 9.

Page 14
33 - 5 = 28

Page 16
8 - 1 = 7
7 - 1 = 6

6 - 1 = 5
5 - 1 = 4
4 - 1 = 3
3 - 1 = 2
2 - 1 = 1
Kit will have none (0)!

Page 17
11 - 1 = 10
20 - 1 = 19
24 - 1 = 23
13 - 1 = 12
21 - 1 = 20
32 - 1 = 31
1 - 1 = 0
100 - 1 = 99
101 - 1 = 100

Page 18
4 - 1 = 3
6 - 2 = 4
10 - 5 = 5
8 - 4 = 4
9 - 6 = 3

10 - 3 = 7
4 - 3 = 1

Page 19
9 - 2 = 7
10 - 8 = 2
26 - 5 = 21
8 - 7 = 1
32 - 3 = 29

68 - 9 = 59
22 - 2 = 20
13 - 5 = 8
80 - 7 = 73

Page 20
2 birds are left.
Claudius has 4 toys.
If you take 5 from 6,
you get 1.
INCREASE does not
mean subtract (it
means add).

Page 21
12 muddy paw prints
are left.
Kit has 7 lives.
Claudius has 5.
9 decreased by 3 is 6.
If you subtract 1 from
6, you get 5.

Page 22
11 + 3 = 14
90 - 2 = 88
5 + 5 = 10
18 + 8 = 26
3 - 3 = 0

Whiz-Bang will be
holding 1 wand.
He will have
15 potions.

**Page 23**
Merlin has 5 berries left.
10 - 3 - 2 = 5
Merlin needs to find
13 more.
There will be 17 with 3
steps and 21 with 7 steps.

**Page 25**
9 + 1 = 10
3 + 7 = 10
5 + 5 = 10
6 + 4 = 10
8 + 2 = 10

**Page 26**

| 8 | 2 | 10 |

| 6 | 4 | 10 |

| 3 | 7 | 10 |

**Page 27**
7 + 3 = 10
5 + 5 = 10
2 + 8 = 10
9 + 1 = 10
7 + 3 = 10
5 + 5 = 10
1 + 9 = 10
6 + 4 = 10
6 + 4 = 10
8 + 2 = 10

**Page 28**
10 - 8 = 2
10 - 4 = 6
10 - 3 = 7
10 - 5 = 5
10 - 9 = 1

**Page 29**
10 - 2 = 8
10 - 5 = 5
10 - 3 = 7
10 - 8 = 2
10 - 7 = 3
10 - 9 = 1
10 - 8 = 2
10 - 4 = 6
10 - 5 = 5
10 - 1 = 9

**Page 30**
Blacktooth has 12 tens.
A 5 is left over.
He needs 4 cannonballs.
He has 7 left.

**Page 31**

| 5 | 5 | 10 |

| 9 | 1 | 10 |

6 + 4
9 + 1
7 + 3

10 - 3 = 7
10 - 2 = 8
10 - 1 = 9

**Page 33**
5 + 6 = 11
5 + 4 = 9

**Page 34**
20 = 10 + 10
12 = 6 + 6
10 = 5 + 5
6 = 3 + 3
16 = 8 + 8

8 = 4 + 4
14 = 7 + 7
2 = 1 + 1
18 = 9 + 9

**Page 35**
6 - 4 = 2

**Page 36**
8 + 8 = 16
8 + 7 = 15
10 + 10 = 20
10 + 11 = 21
3 + 3 = 6
3 + 4 = 7
5 + 5 = 10
6 + 5 = 11
7 + 7 = 14
6 + 7 = 13

**Page 37**
12 = 6 + 6
13 = 6 + 7
2 = 1 + 1
3 = 1 + 2
4 = 2 + 2
5 = 2 + 3
10 = 5 + 5
9 = 5 + 4
8 = 4 + 4
7 = 4 + 3
80 = 40 + 40
70 = 40 + 30

**Page 38**
The ship's cat is 12.
The other parrots were
8 gold coins.
It takes 16 seconds to fly
there and back.

**Page 39**
9 + 10 = 19
The pizza has 6 slices.

Pete gets 5
peanuts and 10
seeds.

**Page 40**
10 - 2 = 8
4 + 6 = 10
3 + 7 = 10
10 - 1 = 9
10 - 5 = 5

1 and 8 do not add up
to 10.

| 2 | 8 | 10 |

**Page 41**
Blacktooth is left with
10 diamonds, 9 rubies,
4 sapphires, and 7
emeralds.
It takes Pete 6 hours.
11 + 10 = 21

# ANSWERS

## Page 43
28
45
56

## Page 44
23 + 10 = 33
42 + 10 = 52
10 + 57 = 67
10 + 51 = 61
64 + 10 = 74
43 + 10 = 53

## Page 45
67 - 10 = 57
18 - 10 = 8
21 - 10 = 11
33 - 10 = 23
49 - 10 = 39
82 - 10 = 72

## Page 46
Bella has 45 petals.
The total of 20 and 10 is 30.
56 is five tens and six units.
Bertie stays for 17 days.

## Page 47
There are 43 bugs in total.
There would be 33 left.
There would be 23 left.
They would buy 20 lollipops.

## Page 48
The missing totals are:
30
50
70
90

## Page 49
110 + 90 = 200

## Page 50
110 + 50 = 160
200 + 200 = 400
110 + 10 = 120
160 + 30 = 190
210 + 70 = 280
120 + 60 = 180
300 + 40 = 340
190 + 20 = 210

## Page 51
120 - 20 = 100
650 - 200 = 450
270 - 50 = 220
150 - 40 = 110
340 - 30 = 310
20 - 20 = 0
330 - 110 = 220

## Page 52
The farmer has 10 eggs left.
He has 5 containers with 50 eggs.
He has 30 eggs left.
Three tens and three tens make 60.

350 is three hundreds and five tens.
80 + 100 + 10 = 190
70 - 30 is different.

## Page 55
6 + 13 doesn't add up to 20.

## Page 56
17 + 3 = 20
16 + 4 = 20
1 + 19 = 20
5 + 15 = 20
18 + 2 = 20
22 + 8 = 30

## Page 57
20 - 6 = 14
20 - 7 = 13
20 - 9 = 11
20 - 8 = 12
20 - 10 = 10
11 and 8 do not add up to 20.

## Page 59
The answer is 3.

## Page 60
The differences are 4 and 6.
2 more blue fish are needed.

## Page 61
4 pairs have a difference of 5.
The sequences end in:
9 (a difference of 2)
4 (a difference of 3)
16 (the differences go up 1, 2, 3, 4).

The difference between
14 and 17 is 3
18 and 6 is 12
2 and 9 is 7.

## Page 62
Sid's dad has been to 2 more islands.
Sid has 8 more teeth.
B needs 4.
C needs 5.

## Page 63
There are 19 dolphins.
The new difference is 3.
Sid swims the second half 5 seconds slower.
The sequence ends in 35 (the differences are 1, 2, 3, 4, 5).

## Page 64
The difference between the bottles is 5.
30 coins will balance the scales.
Hattie has laid 3 more.

## Page 65
90 laps in total.
41 and 8 would end in 9.

ANSWERS

**Page 66**
11 + 13 = 24

**Page 67**
29 + 19 = 48

**Page 68**
24 + 15 = 39
82 + 16 = 98
18 + 11 = 29
23 + 23 = 46
31 + 24 = 55
55 + 14 = 69
57 + 22 = 79
21 + 42 = 63
66 + 33 = 99
79 + 11 = 90

**Page 69**
29 + 29 = 58
39 + 19 = 58
49 + 39 = 88
109 + 29 = 138
59 + 19 = 78
19 + 69 = 88
79 + 19 = 98
49 + 49 = 98
29 + 49 = 78
19 + 18 = 37

**Page 70**
26 - 15 = 11

**Page 71**
90 - 21 = 69

**Page 72**
36 - 25 = 11
28 - 11 = 17
67 - 31 = 36
32 - 12 = 20

54 - 22 = 32
97 - 86 = 11
79 - 52 = 27
21 - 10 = 11
44 - 13 = 31
85 - 23 = 62
101 - 91 = 10

**Page 73**
70 - 19 = 51
60 - 29 = 31
30 - 19 = 11
100 - 89 = 11
80 - 21 = 59
50 - 31 = 19
40 - 11 = 29
100 - 11 = 89

**Page 75**
92 - 75 = 5 + 10 + 2 = 17
81 - 38 = 2 + 40 + 1 = 43
74 - 57 = 3 + 10 + 4 = 17

**Page 76**
69 sips in total.
Georgie leaves 11 more
footprints than Zee.
Georgie eats 35 less in
summer.

**Page 77**
There are 21 males.
There are 25 young ones.
There are 50 adults.
The elephants are beating
the zebras by 24 points.
They are beating the
giraffes by 36 points.
Yes, they are beating both
teams put together.

**Page 79**

299     746

**Page 80**

857     787

653 +
33 +
12 =
―――
698

**Page 81**

356

317 +
60 +
2 =
―――
379

466 +
12 +
1 =
―――
479

555 +
31 +
100 =
―――
686

805 +
23 +
20 =
―――
848

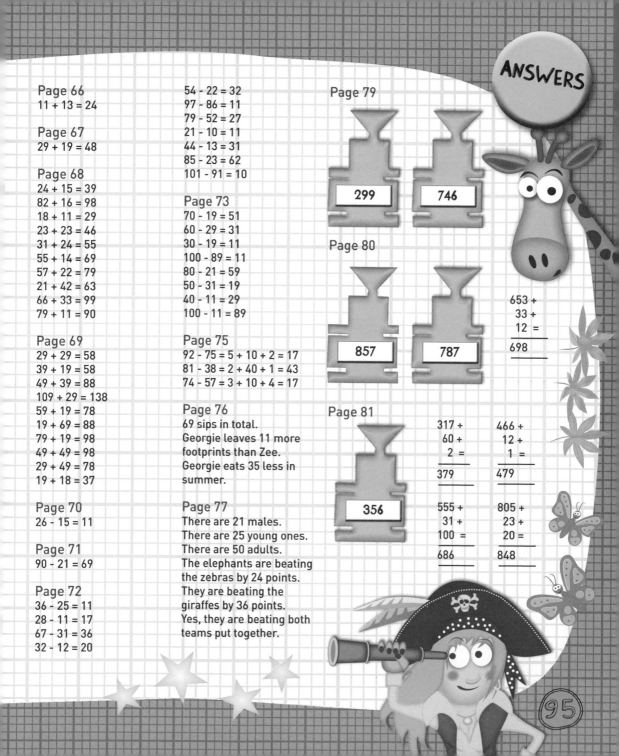

95

# ANSWERS

## Page 82
65 + 12 = 77
72 - 61 = 11
70 + 22 = 92
55 + 25 = 80
87 - 64 = 23
33 + 33 = 66

69 + 69 = 138
59 + 49 = 108
109 + 29 = 138

30 - 21 = 9
90 - 39 = 51
100 - 51 = 49
They have 99 feathers.

## Page 83
62 - 47 = 3 + 10 + 2 = 15

207 +
602 +
 80 =
———
889

554

## Page 85
50¢ - 40¢ = 10¢
15¢ + 15¢ + 25¢ = 55¢   The change is 5¢.

## Page 87

| 2 COOL CONES | 30¢ |
| 2 TASTY CONES | 40¢ |
| 1 YUMMY CUP | 25¢ |
| 1 T-BONE | 25¢ |
| TOTAL | $1.20 |
| CHANGE | 30¢ |

| 1 T-BONE | 25¢ |
| 1 YUMMY CUP | 25¢ |
| TOTAL | 50¢ |
| CHANGE | 50¢ |

You could buy 6 ice creams.

## Page 88
40¢
$1.10
Option 1: 5¢ change
Option 2: no change

## Page 89
75¢
25¢
Total $4.00
He has $1.10 left.

## Page 90
3 + 6 = 9     9 + 2 = 11     10 + 7 = 17     5 + 5 = 10

TIMES has nothing to do with subtraction.

Half of 20 is 10.   Double 8 is 16.

60 - 20 = 40     20 + 10 = 30     10 + 35 = 45

The difference between 10 and 15 is 5.

## Page 91
78 + 11 = 89
100 - 80 = 20
68 + 2 = 70
65 - 35 = 30
92 - 71 = 21
44 - 13 = 31

You can buy 3 ice creams
with 15¢ change.

All 4 pairs have a difference of 8.

240 +
 34 +
202 =
———
476

103 - 77 = 3 + 20 + 3 = 26